Whale Tales

and Other

Animal Stories

Based on the animal adventures of

Michele and Drew Delgross

Professional Animal Trainers

Illustrations by Dana Keith

First published by Dog Ear Publishing
4011 Vincennes Rd
Indianapolis, IN 46268
www.dogearpublishing.net

ISBN: 978-0-9976-7590-0

This book is printed on acid-free paper.

This book is a work of fiction. Places, events, and situations
in this book are purely fictional and any resemblance to actual persons,
living or dead, is coincidental.

Printed in the United States of America

Authors: Michele and Drew Delgross

MADDAnimalTraining@gmail.com

www.PetStateU.com

Illustrations: Dana Keith

Thank You!

Thank you to Everyone who helped us
with these stories……..

To our family members who supported us.
To our co-workers who worked with us
side-by-side and protected us.
To all the guests who came out and cheered us on.
And a special thank you to all the animals
we've worked with – we loved the time we spent with you all -
you've taught us so much about happiness
and showing us that staying positive
is the key to great training!

Thanks to Lewis Delgross, Drew's father
and an English teacher/professor for over 40yrs.,
for the literary input and editing advice!
To all our family members & friends who read the books
and gave us input – we really appreciate it.
To Shannon and the Writer's Guild at the Nordonia Library.
And of course to Miss Valenti's 4th grade class – for their input from our target
audience's point-of-view ☺

Thanks to all our friends and family members, to even guests,
who sent us pictures – there were too many pictures to use them all in the making
of these books, and in all honesty, we can't remember who gave us what pictures –
we have boxes and boxes of them.
But special thanks to Dandi, Linda, Jeff, Amy, another Jeff, Mandy, and Heather
for contributing with some awesome pics!

We love you all –
Michele and Drew

Welcome to Whale Tales

And Other Animal Stories.

Michele and Drew invite you to come along
as they share some of their favorite memories.

These stories and adventures come from
over 50+ years of interacting and playing with a variety
of animals from around the world.

They are blessed to have lived their dreams,
and as some would say, "swim w/the big fish".

Read a little, learn a little, and smile a lot!

<u>Ocean Bay Marine Life Park</u>

Ocean Bay is a fictional place, though it's based on the many zoological & marinelife parks Michele and Drew have worked at, consulted with, and visited over their combined 50+ yrs. in the Animal Industry.   Ocean Bay is the best of all the Parks, Zoos, and Aquariums they've been to......   Ocean Bay is:

Interactive

Beautiful

Exciting

Educational

Fun

Tranquil

Table of Contents:

Teagan

The Killer Whale

"Finds a Buried Treasure"

Based on the animal adventures of

Michele and Drew Delgross

Professional Animal Trainers

It was a beautiful, sunny day at the Ocean Bay Marine Park, and Michele and Drew were doing a show in front of 4,000 guests, with some of their Killer Whale Friends ....

Their names were Teagan,
and his sister Little Denali.

Teagan was 7 yrs. old,
while Denali just turned 3yrs. old.

In the back pools were Teagan and Little Denali's mother, Aurora, and their father, Chogan – playing with their trainers.

All the whales took turns doing shows, and then playing in the back pools – it's a way Michele, Drew, and the other trainers keep the whales active and happy!

Michele and Drew just got done doing a segment with two of the whales, where they all jumped in and out of the water, doing team behaviors to a fun song...

At the end
of the
swimming part
of the show,
Michele and Drew
ended up the side of the pool,
turned around, and hugged the Whales.

The crowd went wild with applause when they were
done, and the whales seemed to enjoy all the
attention from both Michele, Drew, and the guests
sitting in the stands!

Michele then took Little Denali to one side of the
pool, while Drew went to the other side with Teagan.

They each selected a friend from the audience – to
go and meet the killer whale stars!

Michele picked three children,
while Drew found a young newlywed bride.

Michele started her segment
with the kids by jumping up and down,
waving, and doing other fun behaviors,
while Little Denali copied the children.

Again, the crowd was clapping
for the kids and for Little Denali –
everyone was very happy!

Drew and Teagan were with their volunteer,
  and the young lady was rubbing down
  Teagan on his back, just like scratching a dog,

when all of a sudden Teagan left Drew
and the volunteer and went to the bottom
of the pool ………

And stayed down there
for almost a minute!

Drew explained to the audience that Teagan was free to do what he wanted to do and all he was going to do is ignore Teagan's incorrect behavior.

About a minute later, Teagan came up from the bottom of the 33 foot deep pool and sat in front of Drew and the volunteer.

Drew was just about to go on
with the segment when all of a sudden
Teagan opened his mouth, and something "shiny" was
in Teagan's mouth - what could it be...........??

Drew was a little confused by a shiny object in Teagan's mouth, but the killer whales were all taught to bring back strange objects that fell into the pool. Maybe Teagan was simply bring back a rock or something.

But when Drew reached
into the back of Teagan's tongue,
Drew was very surprised at what he found...........

It was a diamond ring!

Drew was just sitting there, pondering
the ring in his hand, when the volunteer
next to him spoke up and said,

"oh, there's my engagement ring!"

Drew was stunned that the woman had lost
her ring and didn't say anything.   More amazing was
that Teagan heard the ring drop while they were
rubbing him down, and he knew enough to get it, and
bring it back to Drew!

Wow!

Drew was impressed and when
he told the audience the story –
everyone cheered for Teagan!

Drew gave Teagan a hug and a huge bucket
of fish to reward him for getting the ring
and bringing it back!

Everything seemed okay, for now………

But when Drew ended the segment
on the side of the pool with the volunteer,
and was saying goodbye to her,
she leaned over and whispered,

"but what about my wedding ring…?"

Ocean Bay
Marine Life Park

What wedding ring...??

Drew looked back a little confused,

not understanding the question,

since Teagan brought back

her engagement ring............

It was then, that he realized

she not only lost her diamond ring,

she also lost her actual wedding ring too!

Holy whale!   There's another ring

at the bottom of the pool...

That's why Teagan
was at the bottom so long –
he was trying to pick up both rings!

Drew explained to the audience
what was going on, and then grabbed
a diving mask, he hopped on Teagan
and went all the way to the bottom of the pool !

There he stayed for about 30 seconds,
searching for the wedding ring.   And then he
saw it in the corner at the bottom of the pool.

He swam over to it with Teagan,
who was having fun just watching
Drew swim down there, and then
they both came up!

POW!

They broke the water's surface,
he raised his hand in the air to
show everyone the second ring!

The crowd went crazy, and everyone
was clapping and cheering!

Michele jumped in the water with Denali, to join Drew and Teagan....

and all four
of them played
in the middle of the pool
for the next
five minutes
with toys,

water jets, hoses, and ...

and lots,

and lots .....

and lots of fish!

Together, Teagan and Little Denali
could eat over 200lbs of fish each day...

While their parents, Aurora and Chogan,
could eat almost 400lbs!

Michele and Drew then ended the show,
and kissed Teagan & Little Denali
goodnight –
they had enough
excitement
for one day.....

Because they knew tomorrow, the whales
would find them more "treasures" –
at Ocean Bay ☺

The End

Sandee
the Manatee

"Playing Hide-n-Seek
on Moving Day"

Based on the animal adventures of

Michele and Drew Delgross

(Professional Animal Trainers)

Illustrated by *Dana Keith*

19

It was a lazy, sunny day at the Ocean Bay
Marine Park, and Drew was working with
the dolphins and whales, while Michele
was performing with the sea lions, walruses,
and otters.

All of a sudden, a phone call came in –
there was a manatee that needed to be brought
back to Ocean Bay, and Drew was asked to go
with a team of animal experts to pick her up.

Her name was Sandee the Manatee;
she was 11 feet long
and weighed over 1,500 pounds.

Sandee was injured a year ago when a boat hit her,
but a team of Veterinarians and Animal Care experts
that worked with Drew, helped Sandee get better.

She was staying at a rescue place
called "Recess Lagoon."

"Recess Lagoon" was such a great place;
blue water, warm breezes, and big beautiful rocks at
the bottom of the sea.

Sandee loved it down there, but now she had to
come back to Ocean Bay since she
was healthy, to make room at Recess Lagoon
for other injured manatees.

Drew and the team of animal experts arrived
at Recess Lagoon in the early afternoon.

There they saw Sandee
playing with four other manatees
that were recovering from injuries too.

One was eating lettuce,

two were playing "tag" with Sandee,

and the last one was sleeping

near a pelican.

But when they saw all the humans

standing at the beach staring at them,

they ducked under the water

and hid behind the big rocks

and sea grasses at the bottom

of the sea pen!

It was supposed to be a quick trip,
and the animal team planned on getting
Sandee and coming home all in one day...

But Sandee had different plans!

Drew and all the animal people gathered

that next morning and talked about how

they were going to capture Sandee......

lift her up with a big crane,

and then put her in the big box truck

they drove down.

The truck was like a large refrigerator
that kept cold, and they had a soft bed
of foam for Sandee to lie on,
so she would be comfortable.

Everything seemed perfect on land –
but things changed
when they got in the water!

The first twenty minutes went according
to the plan;   A large net surrounded Sandee
and the other manatees.

And then, one-by-one the animal team released the
other four manatees, leaving only Sandee.

They thought they would be home
        by dinner time – it was too simple.
                And then it happened ....

Sandee didn't want to leave Recess Lagoon
or her Manatee friends!

For the next eleven hours, Sandee dodged,
ducked, hid, and laughed at the ten animal experts,
including Drew, while she got away from the net
each time they surrounded her!

By the end of the first day, Drew and his animal
team had to quit because night-time was upon them.

They had tried 22 times to catch Sandee,
and failed to grab her every single time!

All the animal people went back to the hotel
and took hot showers.   They were tired,
hungry, and wanted to get the salt off them.

But Sandee and her manatee friends
didn't mind, because when Drew left the sea pen,
he looked back and saw four of the manatees playing
tag in the warm water, and there was Sandee, eating
her dinner of lettuce .....

Sandee could eat almost 100 pounds
of vegetables a day!

When Drew and the team returned
the next morning, they tried the same plan
as the day before.

They would surround Sandee with the net,
watch her go under the water, and again,
they would watch her "pop up" on the
other side of the sea pen!

But at one point, halfway through the day,
something happened, and it changed the way
they were pulling the net!

Around Noon, Drew had volunteered
to SCUBA dive the bottom of the sea pen,
to help drag the net over the large rocks,
and when he was down there, something happened......

At one point he was moving the net over a large
rock, when all of a sudden, the rock "squealed"!

Squealed like a pig!

This not only startled Drew, it scared him too –
because rocks don't "squeal", do they……..?

But the rock was really Sandee!
She had been diving to the bottom
of the sea pen and "acting" like a rock!

So when they were dragging and pulling
the nets over the rocks, they were accidently
letting Sandee go to the other side!

Wow!

Drew swam to the surface of the water
and shouted to the others what was happening...

Sandee was playing Hide-n-Seek
behind the rocks!

The crew all gathered at the beach,
going over a "new" plan on how to collect

Sandee – a super smart manatee,
who had wasted two days
by playing hide-n-seek.

Now, with their new plan,
adding a net to the bottom,
they had Sandee within twenty minutes
and were moving her to the beach!

Once on the beach, they picked
Sandee up with the crane,
loaded her into the truck,
packed it with a bunch of ice
to keep her cool,
and started driving towards Ocean Bay.

Sandee's game of hide-n-seek
had made them two days late,
but they arrived safely six hours later.

And when they lowered Sandee into
the water of her new Manatee home,
all the other manatees came over
and greeted her with hugs and kisses.

They became friends quickly!

Soon, they were all playing a game
of manatee tag, all except Sandee……

She looked over at Drew – and slowly swam
over to him.   He patted her on the nose one last
time, handed her some lettuce, and watched
her gently glide away to enjoy her dinner.

And all he could think in his mind was,
'tag, you're it Sandee, until next time'….

The End

Karlee

The Special Bird

from the Spice Islands

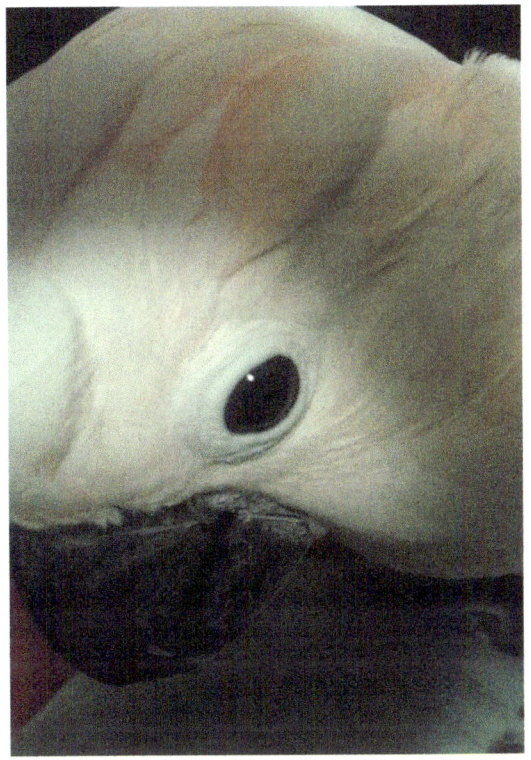

"Meets a New Friend"

Based on the animal adventures of

Michele and Drew Delgross

Professional Animal Trainers

It was a lazy, sunny day at the Ocean Bay
Marine Park.   Drew was swimming
with the dolphins and whales,

while Michele was playing with the
sea lions, walruses, and otters.

When all of a sudden a phone call came in -
there was a sick bird that needed help,
and Michele and Drew were asked to come to
the Bird Barn to see what they could do.

When they got to the Bird Barn they saw
a big, pink Cockatoo with broken,
ugly feathers and a doctor's cone
around her neck.

Her name was Karlee
and she needed their help.

Karlee was a Cockatoo whose family
was from the Spice Islands,
which is near Australia.

Karlee was shy because she had never learned
how to play and make friends.   Around other
birds, she would run away
or scream and squawk at them.

Sometimes, when really upset,
she would pull out her own feathers -
ouch!

Karlee was a very sick bird –
and needed help!

Drew and Michele had done a lot of teaching and caring for sick animals, everything from feeding tiny baby otters and penguins, to giving shots

to sick dolphins, to even treating killer whales with toothaches.

But working with a shy, sick Cockatoo from the Spice Islands was a first.

This was going to be something
new for Michele and Drew,
and Karlee too.

When Michele and Drew first took Karlee back to their area they could tell she was scared because she wouldn't look at them.

She was shaking, shivering, and was trying to run away from them.

She couldn't fly because she hadn't had enough feathers on her wings in years.

Karlee wasn't mean, she was just shy
around other animals, and since she was

always sick,
and the doctors
were always fixing
her boo-boos,
that made her
even more upset
around humans!

But this is where Michele and Drew's skills
came into play, because they had lots of practice
teaching different and difficult animals.

They were going to be Karlee's new teachers,
and Karlee was their newest student......

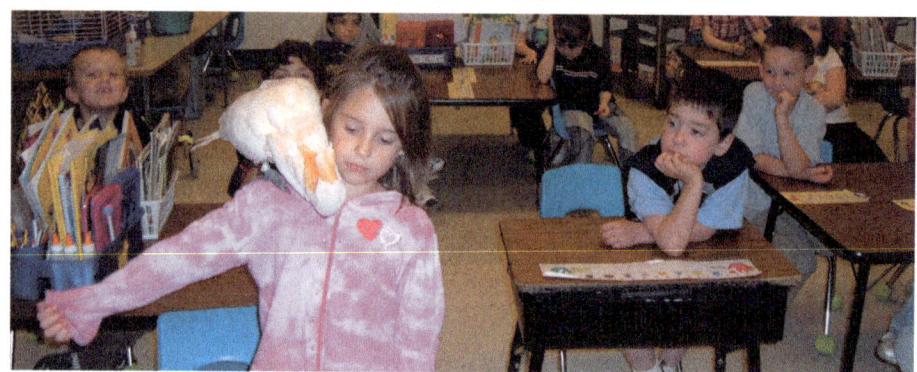

Karlee was going back to school!

Some of the changes Michele and Drew first made were very simple, such as feeding her at different times and hiding her treats in logs and under branches to keep her busy.

This made her use her brain to think plus it gave her some good exercise - something she hadn't had in quite a long time.

Karlee also had to learn new behaviors and how to play with toys.   Yes, even playing with toys has to be taught, and after Karlee learned how to play, she loved it!

Every time she got it right, Karlee got a prize!
And this helped build a loving friendship.

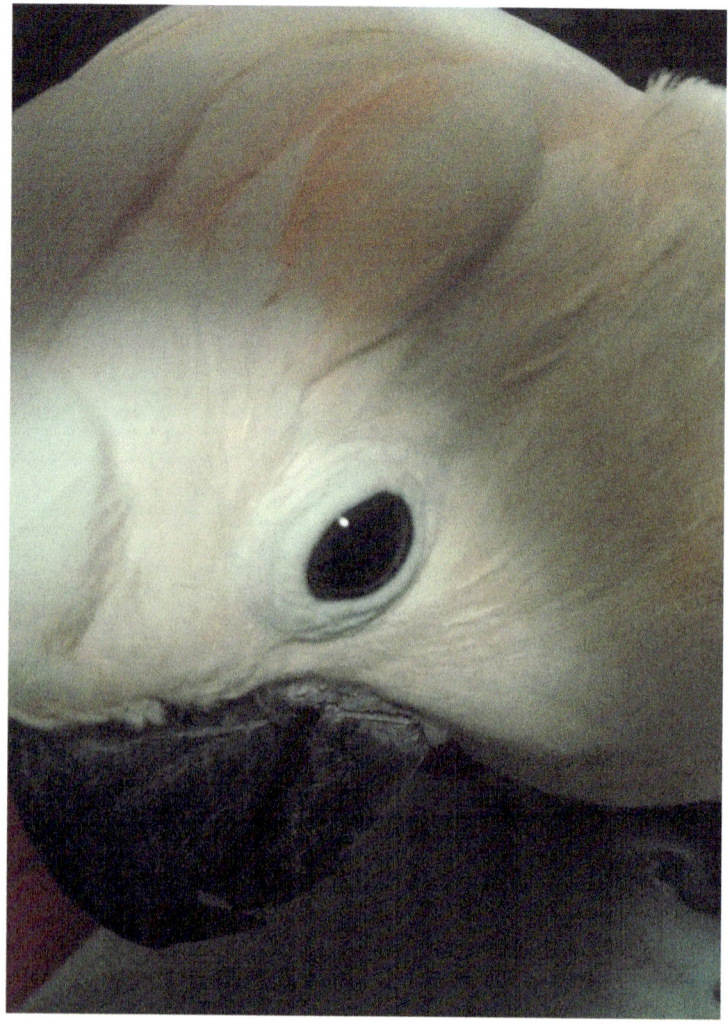

Drew and Michele even helped the doctors become
Karlee's friends.   This made taking care of her
much easier and she was not scared of the doctors
anymore.

Since Karlee was doing so well they wanted to take her on a play-date. Michele and Drew introduced her to a beautiful, white Cockatoo named Charlie.

Charlie's family was from Australia, near where Karlee's family was from.

Karlee was scared when she first met Charlie; she was shaking just like when Michele and Drew first saw Karlee in her cage.

On the other hand, Charlie liked seeing
another bird, since Charlie was born at
Ocean Bay and had grown up with a
group of birds.

After a couple of weeks together,
a bucket full of bird seeds and a lot of love,

Karlee and Charlie became friends!
They got along so well, that after a short time
they even slept in the same cage at night.

Karlee was doing so well with Charlie,
Michele and Drew took her to meet
more birds throughout the Marine Park.

There was Ruby the Flamingo,

and Onyx the Black Palm Cockatoo!

Karlee also met a couple of beautiful Macaws,
their names were Zeus and Athena –
and they loved to mimic their trainer's voices!

During the next year, Karlee went everywhere with
her two favorite humans - even going home
with Michele and Drew to spend the night .

There she would play with Michele and Drew's children, their two dogs and cats ....

It was a zoo at their home, and Karlee and Charlie fit right in!

And each new friend Karlee made, helped her get better – and she stopped hurting herself!

Karlee was always learning new things
with Drew and Michele.   She learned over
thirty (30) new behaviors that first year!

Karlee & Charlie even performed
in parades and TV shows together.

The kids loved the games that Karlee
and Charlie would play, such as waving to them,
screaming on command, and spreading their wings
out like an eagle ☺

Karlee met thousands of people and everyone always cheered for her – she loved it!

Two years after Michele and Drew started teaching Karlee, she had gone from a sick and shy bird to a healthy and happy animal member of the Ocean Bay Marine Park.

Then one night, when Michele and Drew
were saying goodnight to all the birds,
they saw something different in
Karlee and Charlie's cage -
what was it..?

What was Charlie protecting

in their nest....??....

there was an egg!

Wow!

How exciting was this year going to be –
Karlee and Charlie were going to be parents!

Michele and Drew then gave Karlee and Charlie extra hugs and kisses because tomorrow would be another exciting day at Ocean Bay - with the Special Birds from the Spice Islands!

The End

About the Authors:

Michele Delgross

grew up in San Diego, California. Her father was in the U.S. Navy, and growing up in Southern California, Michele participated in a variety of water sports from an early age; like the varsity swim & water polo teams!

After High School, she worked as a San Diego Lifeguard, with her brother, while going to college.

She then started at SeaWorld in San Diego in 1985 in the Entertainment Department. A year later she started in the Animal Training Department working with the dolphins, pilot whales, otters, sea lions, and walruses!

In 1991, Michele moved to Aurora, Ohio, which is near Cleveland, to work for the Sea World of Ohio Park, just for the Summer Show Season. But during that time she fell in love with the Midwest, with its "hometown" venues and values, and it's also where she met Drew!

Over the next 13yrs., as a Senior Trainer in Ohio, Michele lead numerous training areas, working with the killer whales, dolphins, sea lions, otters, walruses, penguins, monkeys, hawks, eagles, and parrots.

Drew Delgross

Started his "animal journey" in Vermilion, Ohio, growing up on Lake Erie. He started swimming at a young age – and by the time he was 16yrs. old, he had already become a certified SCUBA diver and a lifeguard.

He went to Bowling Green State University after High School, studying marine biology and psychology, and then left for the U.S. Navy as a Petty Officer in the Nuclear Power program.

After getting out of the military in Orlando in 1986, he joined the SeaWorld of Florida Park as an Animal Trainer – working w/the dolphins, sea lions, otters, and killer whales.

And then, in 1991, he moved back to his home-state, and there at the Ohio Park, he supervised numerous training areas, including the Whale stadium, the SeaLion & Otter stadium, Patagonia Passage, Dolphin Cove, and even a new Special Events bird/monkey/media area that Michele and him started up together!

Dana Keith
Illustrator / Artist

As a child Dana's family often took her on trips to SeaWorld of Ohio where she developed a sincere love for animals, especially marine life.
From a very young age she wanted to dedicate her life to animals and conservation.

Dana went on to graduate from Kent State University with a Bachelors degree in Psychology in 2011.
After college she pursued working with animals by becoming a certified professional dog trainer.

In 2014 she accepted an internship working with California sea lions at Mystic Aquarium in Mystic, Connecticut and learned about animal husbandry, marine mammal training and conservation.

When Dana returned from Mystic Aquarium she spent her time volunteering for the Akron Zoo and the Medina Raptor Center where she learned and cared for injured and rehabilitated birds of prey.

In 2015 Dana was offered a position at the Akron Zoo.
There she enjoys teaching, animal encounters, and speaking to guests about all of the animals at the zoo.

Dana is a self-taught artist and enjoys painting wildlife in her free time. She claims she gained her experience as an artist by trying to capture the beauty of our oceans with a paintbrush. She hopes her art may inspire children to protect the oceans, conserve our planet and to follow their dreams. Her biggest inspiration is marine life artist, Robert Wyland. Dana lives in North Canton, Ohio with her two dogs, Goober the pug and Suki the Husky.

CPSIA information can be obtained
at www.ICGtesting.com
Printed in the USA
FSOW04n0139161116
27411FS